The Only Way is Ethics

Part 2: Life and Death

Sean Doherty

First published 2016 by Authentic Media Limited,
PO Box 6326, Bletchley, Milton Keynes, MK1 9GG.
authenticmedia.co.uk

British Library Cataloguing in Publication Data
A catalogue record for this book is available from the British Library.
ISBN: 978-1-78078-152-5

Cover design by Sara Garcia

The chapters included in this work 'Hoping for Children', 'Tricky
Decisions at the End of Life', and 'When Does Life Begin?' are
published individually, all copyright © 2016 by Sean Doherty.

Hoping for Children
ISBN 978-1-78078-154-9   978-1-78078-444-1 (e-book)

Tricky Decisions at the End of Life
ISBN 978-1-78078-155-6   978-1-78078-445-8 (e-book)

When Does Life Begin?
ISBN 978-1-78078-153-2   978-1-78078-443-4 (e-book)

CONTENTS

When Does Life Begin?

Abortion

One in three women in the UK, at some point in their life, will have at least one abortion, and the abortion rate is relatively evenly spread amongst women across social, economic and ethnic differences. Abortion is not the preserve of a particular minority group who do not know about or have access to contraception. It is a massive reality in our society and in the lives of many women (and men), yet it is rarely spoken about, especially in churches. Of course, some Christians oppose abortion vocally, and some of them do so in a hurtful way. Most of us, therefore, avoid the subject altogether, not wanting to judge or wound people who are already vulnerable. Rather than discussing abortion in a non-judgemental way, we remain silent.

Although well intended, this silence is damaging. Certain voices come to dominate the public discussion. When people haven't been given the chance to think through the issue of unintended pregnancy in advance, they are more likely to have an abortion. And those who have had abortions can feel more judged, not less, because treating it as a taboo makes it seem shameful and gives them the false impression that abortion doesn't affect others. This adds to feelings of isolation and shame and denies them the chance to name and process their feelings and experiences, whereas an honest conversation could bring acceptance and assurance. Silence might seem better than judgement – but addressing abortion with compassion is better than both.

My hope in what follows is to show that biblical and theological thinking with respect to abortion does not undermine a sensitive and compassionate response. In fact, we need to know what God thinks about abortion in order to respond sensitively and compassionately. I will therefore start with a look at the reality of abortion in our culture today, explore why human life is so precious according to Scripture, and consider when human life begins. On that basis, I'll explain when I think that abortion is legitimate and when it is not.

I cannot say here all that should be said pastorally about abortion. For that, I wholeheartedly recommend a book by Jonathan Jeffes, a trained crisis pregnancy counsellor and leader of an abortion recovery programme, *Abortion: Breaking the Silence in the Church*.[1] I have learnt a huge amount from Jonathan in this area, and his influence shapes what follows.

---

[1] Jonathan Jeffes, *Abortion: Breaking the Silence in the Church* (Chichester: Lean Press, 2013).

Who has abortions and why?

Today, arguments often made in favour of abortion are that it ensures that women are not forced to continue with a pregnancy when a man has committed rape or if the pregnancy places their health or even life in danger, and it protects young teenage girls for whom having children could be physically and emotionally dangerous. It's worth comparing these arguments to the reality of abortion in our society today.

Every year in England and Wales there are more than 190,000 abortions. In 2014, the total number was 190,092. The age at which a woman was most likely to have an abortion was 22. Abortions for girls under the age of 14 accounted for 0.05 per cent of the total, and those under the age of 16 had 1.3 per cent of abortions. That is, 1.3 per cent of abortions were provided for girls who were under the age of sexual consent. The abortion rate amongst girls under the age of 16 is declining.[2]

As is well known, abortion is not automatically available at the woman's request. Two physicians must be satisfied that one or more grounds for an abortion have been met. (In practice, the woman only has to meet one of the doctors.) These grounds are: that the pregnancy constitutes a

---

[2] See https://www.gov.uk/government/uploads/ system/uploads/attachment_data/file/433437/ 2014_Commentary__5_.pdf, pp. 10–11.

threat to the life of the mother, that it could affect her physical or emotional health, that the child would have a serious disability, or that the birth of another child would put the wellbeing of existing children in jeopardy.

In practice, however, this means the following. Fewer than 200 abortions were performed because the mother's life or physical health was in danger. Only 1.7 per cent of abortions are performed because the child would be seriously disabled, and 0.7 per cent are performed to protect the wellbeing of existing children. This means that 97.5 per cent of abortions are provided on the grounds that the mother's physical or mental health is at risk. Of these, 99.93 per cent were reported as being due to a risk to the mother's mental health.[3]

No official data has been gathered detailing the proportion of abortions which took place when the pregnancy resulted from a man committing rape. About 24,000 rapes were officially reported in 2014, the vast majority of which were the rape of a woman by a man. However, the real figure is almost certainly many times higher than that – as many as 85,000, according to one crime survey published in 2007.[4] Studies in the US have established the proportion of rapes that result in pregnancy. Assuming that the rape-related pregnancy rate in the UK is similar, Jonathan Jeffes

---

[3] See previous link, p. 13.

[4] Jeffes, *Abortion: Breaking the Silence*, Appendix 1.

has estimated that perhaps as many as 2 per cent of abortions in the UK take place following rape.

So, we can now give a tentative answer to our question. In 2014, about 0.7 per cent of abortions took place to protect the life or health of the mother, 1.3 per cent were for girls under the age of sexual consent, and maybe another 2 per cent take place when the pregnancy was a result of rape – giving us a rough guesstimate that perhaps about 4 per cent of abortions take place for the reasons often cited in favour of abortion.

One major reason for the prevalence of abortion amongst women over the age of consent, which is not to do with rape or protecting the mother's health or life, is probably our contemporary relationship to contraception. Our age has seen an unparalleled improvement in the effectiveness of contraception. In laboratory conditions, contraceptives such as the pill, the coil and such barrier contraceptives as condoms are nearly 100 per cent effective. Yet despite the ready availability of more effective contraception than humanity has ever before known, half of all women in the UK will experience an unintended pregnancy at some point during their life, and one in three will have at least one abortion.[5] Yet studies have found that the majority of women who have an abortion were using contraception at the

---

[5] Of course, some of these pregnancies will be the result of rape or when a woman has been forced into not using contraception.

time they became pregnant, and that nearly all of them knew about and had ready access to reliable contraception.[6] In other words, contraception is much less effective than we think it is. After all, sex doesn't take place in laboratory conditions! We are much less in control of our own fertility than we think we are – but the illusion of control leaves us unprepared for unintended pregnancy. Thus, the era of effective contraception has, ironically, become the era of abortion.

Another reason why so many people have abortions is that our society (and even the church) makes it far easier for women to terminate an unintended pregnancy than to go ahead with it. Of course, it *is* the woman's choice whether or not to continue with any given pregnancy. But we cannot claim that women have a true choice when the emotional, financial and other costs of raising a child are so high compared to the ready availability of abortion. Imagine how a woman experiencing a crisis pregnancy might feel if she received the following response from her parents, her partner, or the church: 'You would make an excellent mother. If you choose to have the baby, I/we will love and support you through pregnancy and raise the child with you, or support you in putting the child up for adoption if you feel that is the right option for you. If you feel you cannot raise the child, I/we would be very

---

[6] For details of these studies, see Jeffes, *Abortion: Breaking the Silence*, p. 27 and notes 21–23.

happy to raise him or her. Whatever you choose, you will not be alone.' By making the possibility of having the child seem less lonely and genuinely feasible, this approach does not pressurise the woman or limit her range of options, but *increases* them, whereas today many woman who experience a crisis pregnancy *do* feel pressure – to have an abortion.

A sense of limited options can be particularly acute for Christians in churches which (rightly) teach that sex is only for marriage. Although this teaching is good, if it creates a negative environment for unmarried women who become pregnant, they are more likely to seek a secret abortion than let everyone at church find out that they had sex outside marriage.

Let's turn next to why human life is so precious, and the all-important question of when human life begins.

Why is human life so precious?

The Bible doesn't specifically mention abortion. This silence has led some to conclude that it is not wrong. (That assumes that the Bible intends to set out an exhaustive list of every possible sin, which it doesn't.) Others go to the other extreme, quoting a text such as 'You shall not murder' (Exod. 20:13), as if that alone settles the matter. These extremes both make arguments from silence, reading into the text something which it does not directly say. Instead, let's look at Scripture as a whole to see what light it sheds.

We discover in the first creation story (Gen. 1) that humanity is made in God's image. This is why we are precious: because God has made us like God. The value of human life is therefore intrinsic – it is something given to us, something fundamentally true about us, rather than something which we earn through our success, or intelligence, or reaching a particular stage of development and maturity. And if we cannot earn it, we can't lose it either, through sin, or sickness, or the loss of particular faculties.

Because the value of human life is intrinsic and not earned, we may not decide for ourselves that some types of people are more human than others. We are usually appalled at the idea that some people are superior or inferior to others. But we fall into that very trap if we think that some human lives deserve less protection because they are at a very early stage of development, or because they lack consciousness or the ability to reason or make decisions. If we are human, we are made in God's image.

This helps us understand the sixth commandment, 'Do not murder' (Exod. 20:13). It is not arbitrary. Rather, it is based on a particular reason, namely that human life is intrinsically precious because it is made in God's image. Indeed, in Genesis 9:6, Scripture explicitly explains that innocent human life should not be taken, precisely because humanity is made in the image of God.[7]

This explains why the command not to murder is expressed in such absolute, non-negotiable terms. We cannot make exceptions to the principle that we should not take innocent human life, because no human beings are exceptions to the principle that humans are precious to God and made in God's image. Thus, abortion cannot be justified, at least from a Christian perspective, by the claim that it is the lesser of two evils, the best possible or the least awful outcome in tragic circumstances. I will explain further below why I do not believe that the end justifies the means.

When does human life begin?

Knowing that human life is precious and should not be harmed does not, on its own, settle anything regarding abortion. Why should a tiny clump

---

[7] I say 'innocent human life' because the Old Testament permits, and sometimes demands, the taking of human life in certain circumstances, namely war and capital punishment. Most Christians today, of course, are opposed to capital punishment, and many Christians are even pacifists. This is because, if anything, the New Testament strengthens and intensifies the Old Testament emphasis on the preciousness of human life. It certainly does not weaken it.

of cells be awarded the same level of protection and care as a fully developed human being?

Several biblical texts are often quoted to answer this question. The most famous is Psalm 139:13–14, which puts it this way:

> For you formed my inward parts;
>> you knitted me together in my mother's womb.
> I praise you, for I am fearfully and wonderfully made.

God cares for human life so much that he works on us even before we are born. Again, this is what makes human life so precious, because we are knitted together by God, patiently and lovingly. Our preciousness is bestowed on us as a gift from God – and nobody can take it away from us.

But this verse does not say more than it says – that is, it doesn't intend to tell us *when* that process of knitting together takes place. Does it start at the moment of fertilisation, and carry on throughout pregnancy? Or does it begin early on in pregnancy, when the nervous system starts to emerge, or perhaps at a more advanced stage, such as viability or quickening (when the mother can start to feel the baby kick and move around)?

Although Psalm 139 doesn't answer this question, several other biblical texts do point to a specific moment at which human life begins. In Job 3:3, as part of Job's lament over the horrific suffering he has experienced, he curses the night that he was conceived. Of course, the Hebrew word translated 'conceived' cannot be taken absolutely to mean 'the moment the sperm and egg came together', because that would assume far more scientific precision than was known at the time. But the fact that it took place at night presumably refers to the time his parents slept together and thereby conceived him.

We find a similar idea in Psalm 51:5. Elsewhere in the Old Testament, the Hebrew word translated 'conceived' always refers to animals mating (e.g. Gen. 30:38–41). The underlying view here is that life begins when conception takes place, following the sexual union of the parents.

The same view is evident in the New Testament, in the story of the Annunciation. Gabriel tells Mary, 'you will conceive . . . and bear a son, and you shall call his name Jesus' (Luke 1:31, and see also Matt. 1:20). Again, the Greek word for 'conceive' is not intended in scientific terms to refer to the fertilisation of an egg by a sperm. But it points to life beginning very early on, when Mary becomes pregnant.

Whilst these texts do not speak scientifically, they all assume that human life begins at the beginning of pregnancy. Conception is not the beginning of something which becomes a person later on – it is the beginning of that person. As John Stott puts it, these verses witness to a personal continuity between embryo or foetus as it grows in the womb, and the fully developed adult. The unborn child and the adult are the same person, albeit at different stages of development. Stott therefore concludes that, 'The foetus is neither a growth in the mother's body, nor even a potential human being, but already a human being who, though not yet mature, has the potentiality of growing into the fullness of the individual humanity he already possesses.'[8]

Why is this? How can a tiny clump of cells be a person (albeit a small and not yet fully developed one)? The answer is that the biblical writers assume that *personal* human life begins when *physical* human life begins. This is explained by the creation story in Genesis 2, when Adam is fashioned from 'the dust of the earth' into a physical human being (Gen. 2:7). That is, human beings are not created as disembodied spirits, or as physical beings that are animated by a soul which is added on at a later stage. The church rejected this idea when it rejected the heresy of Gnosticism, which taught that inside some human beings there is imprisoned a divine spark which needs to be released from its nasty, physical prison. By contrast, Genesis 1 and 2 describe humans as physical, bodily creatures, and says that this is a good thing.

The goodness of this embodied existence is supremely affirmed in the incarnation, life, resurrection and ascension of Jesus. God thinks our bodies are so good that God gets one for himself! Jesus dignifies our bodies by taking bodily nature onto himself, and he hallows it even

---

[8] John Stott, *Abortion* (Marshalls Paperbacks: 1984), p. 16. Emphasis mine.

further by ascending bodily to his Father. Human life *is* bodily life.

This implies that our lives as people begin when our physical life begins – that is, at the moment of fertilisation. Fertilisation is when a new human life begins physically. A fertilised egg is not a part of the mother or the father in the way that the sperm and egg were – something new has begun. No new beginning takes place after this: all that ensues is the natural development of the new life which has already begun. Significant milestones such as the emergence of the primitive streak, organ development, quickening, viability and birth are clearly developments towards maturity, not the beginning from scratch of something new.[9]

---

[9] It is sometimes claimed that because identical twinning and, more unusually, the accidental fusion of two fertilised embryos into one can take place any time up until fourteen days after conception, the embryo is not really a new person until then. I find this argument strange because in embryos who do not divide at this point, nothing magical happens at fourteen days that brings a life into being which wasn't there before. This view also has to explain why twinning suddenly creates two new lives where there wasn't even one previously. It seems more credible to me to say that twinning is the remarkable process of one life becoming two, rather than one non-life suddenly becoming two lives.

Approaches which conclude that embryos are not people work from the assumption that being a person entails, for example, the ability to think, feel or make decisions, or perhaps the quality of independence and being able to fend for oneself. The dangerous outcome of this way of thinking is that we will tend not to give the same level of care and protection to people who lack these qualities. If you believe that human life only ought to be protected once it has rationality, sentience, will, or some other trait, it's that trait which you think worth protecting, not human life as such. But, as we saw above, being human is not an achievement based on having certain capacities, but comes from being made in God's image.

We can see that being human is about more than possessing traits such as sentience and rationality from the fact that some people do not possess some of these traits – but they are clearly still people! Some severely mentally disabled people may not be able to make rational decisions, but they are still people. (And computers can process information rationally, but they are not.) Some people have a condition called congenital anaesthesia, which prevents them from feeling any pain. So it can't be sentience which makes us human. Someone who is unconscious, perhaps due to a general anaesthetic, is still human – so it can't be consciousness either. And all small children and many infirm adults (for example, people on kidney dialysis) are utterly dependent for survival on care from outside of themselves. So, we can't say that the foetus is only worthy of protection once it becomes independent. In fact, vulnerable dependence on others is an essential part of being human.

This array of possibilities demonstrates that one's view of when human life begins depends on the answer to the question of what it is that makes us human: the ability to think, or make decisions, or independence. As we have seen, the biblical picture of humanity does not privilege these 'higher' human functions, because it assumes that the physical beginning of human bodily life is the beginning of that person's life, because we are fundamentally physical, bodily creatures, and not simply spiritual ones.

This means that we cannot pinpoint a time when personal life begins, other than when human bodily life begins. An embryo may indeed lack sentience, rationality and autonomy – but it is a new, living human being, and it becomes this at the moment of its conception. It is simply a very immature human being at a very early stage of development. It is a new bodily life, which means it is a new person, and therefore made in God's image and precious to God.

There is a surprisingly simple answer to the question, 'Why should a clump of cells be protected like any other human being?' What are human beings *except* clumps of cells, at varying degrees of development or deterioration? No extra, spiritual bit is added that makes us truly human. When a new bodily life begins, so does a new person.

If this is so, human life should be protected from harm from the time that it begins physically until the time that it ends physically. This view, grounded in the picture of what makes us human given in Genesis 2, explains and is corroborated by the biblical texts we discussed which regard life as beginning at the start of pregnancy, resulting from the sexual union of the parents.

How should we respond if we aren't sure when life begins?

Most theologians and Christian traditions today therefore conclude that life begins at conception, and should be nurtured and protected from destruction from that point onwards, and that deliberately destroying such life is therefore wrong in nearly all circumstances. But even if someone is not convinced that life begins at conception, there is a further reason to treat embryos *as if* they are human.

Here's why. The development of the embryo is gradual. At no objective point other than conception can we say that a human life has come into existence that did not exist before that moment. Because human life is so precious, and its destruction so terrible, if we think there is a possibility that a human life is at stake, we have to err on the safe side. That is, we should treat embryos as people unless we have proof that they are not.

Let's use a fictional scenario to illustrate. Pretend that a particular construction worker has the responsibility for demolishing a building using controlled explosives. They must first ensure that no people are inside the building when they initiate the detonation, because anyone inside would be killed or seriously injured. The destruction of human life (even accidentally and unintentionally) is so serious that we recognise our obligation to proactively prevent it.

Now let's pretend that, in the scenario, the worker learns that someone might be inside the building, despite the 'Keep Out' notices plastered everywhere. The worker is now in a situation of uncertainty as to whether human lives are at risk. That uncertainty does not give them a carefree *carte blanche* to proceed with the job. Quite the opposite: the uncertainty creates an obligation to hold back. Human life is so precious that the worker would be culpable if they proceeded without first checking the building thoroughly. If someone died, it would not be murder – the deliberate taking of an innocent human life – but they would still be seriously at fault. They must be sure that a human life is not at stake *before* they proceed.

Personally, I think that Scripture shows that human life begins at the moment of conception. Not everyone is convinced. But, just like our construction worker, if you are not convinced, that does not mean you can go ahead when a human being might be destroyed. Rather, you must err on the side of caution. The burden of proof falls on those who wish to prove that deliberate destruction of an embryo or foetus is permissible – equivalent in my fictional scenario to checking the building and ensuring that nobody is inside.

To summarise, if embryos are human beings from the moment of conception but we fail to realise it, the result in terms of the destruction of innocent human life is horrendous. Therefore, in the absence of proof beyond reasonable doubt that life begins later than conception, we must treat embryos *as if* they are humans from that moment.[10]

Is abortion right in any circumstances?

I believe that abortion is a legitimate step to take in at least one situation, and that is where the pregnancy has placed the life of the mother in jeopardy. For example, ectopic pregnancy (where the embryo implants in the fallopian tube rather

---

[10] This point is developed brilliantly by Robert Song in, 'To Be Willing to Kill What for All One Knows Is a Person Is to Be Willing to Kill a Person', in Brent Waters and Ronald Cole-Turner (eds), *God and the Embryo: Religious Voices on Stem Cells and Cloning* (Washington: Georgetown University Press, 2003), pp. 98–107.

than the womb) will almost certainly lead to the death of the mother (and therefore also of the child, who cannot survive outside the womb at this stage of its development). Part of the trauma and pressure of such a situation is that the choice usually has to be made extremely quickly.

Of course, even in such a perilous situation, some women choose not to have an abortion. They refuse to act to harm their own child, even if that comes at the cost of their own life. This is humbling and deeply admirable, but I don't think it is the only legitimate choice.

There are two bad arguments in favour of abortion to save the mother's life, so first I want to explain why I do not find them convincing.

First, many argue that abortion to save the life of the mother is right because it is an act of self-defence. However, I don't think killing someone in self-defence is a legitimate option, because Jesus teaches us to turn the other cheek (Matt. 5:39). And, even if self-defence is legitimate, a powerless foetus is not the same as someone who is deliberately trying to harm you.

Another unconvincing argument is that abortion to save the mother's life is the lesser of two evils. But faithful Christians cannot employ the consequentialist 'end justifies the means' approach of doing a wrong thing in order to produce good results. This pragmatic approach to ethics is the one adopted by Caiaphas to advocate the execution of Jesus (John 11:50), which isn't a very good advert! And, as Paul puts it,

'Why not do evil that good may come? – as some people slanderously charge us with saying. Their condemnation is just' (Rom. 3:8). If God has prohibited something without exceptions, such as deliberately taking innocent human life because all human life is intrinsically precious, it is not up to us to make exceptions to the command. If we think abortion is legitimate in this situation because it is the lesser of two evils, it will also be legitimate in many other situations.

This leads us to the reason why abortion to save a mother's life can be legitimate. I have said that we cannot make exceptions to God's commands. But this is an occasion when abortion does not break a command. Let me explain.

There are no exceptions to the command, 'Do not murder.' But what is murder? Earlier, I described it as the deliberate taking of innocent human life. In the context of Exodus 20, 'murder' cannot mean 'killing', because war and capital punishment are seen as legitimate.[11] This is why the Christian just war tradition insists that killing in war must be restricted to enemy combatants

---

[11] As noted, though, the Christian tradition has generally been against capital punishment, because it prevents someone from having time to repent and change their ways. So, for example, the Old Testament law required the death penalty for adultery, but Jesus famously saves a woman from this penalty whilst instructing her to 'sin no more' (John 8:11).

and not civilians. Similarly, it is not murder when someone does something which accidentally leads to the death of another person – although they might be culpable of negligence or manslaughter. Hence, murder is the *deliberate* taking of innocent human life.

When it comes to abortion to save the mother's life, the taking of life is not deliberate. It is a consequence which the physician can foresee will happen when he or she intervenes to save the life of the mother – but it is not something that they want or intend to happen. If the child somehow miraculously survived, the physician and mother would be overjoyed – because their intention is not to harm the child. This is quite different to the majority of abortions, which take place precisely so that there will not be a child at the end of the process. That is, the intention or goal in these other cases is to end the life of the child.

This principle is sometimes known as 'double effect'. It says that there is a difference between *foreseeing* the negative consequences of an action, and *intending* those negative consequences. Abortion to save the mother's life has two effects: the saving of one life and the ending of another. You cannot produce the first effect without producing the second effect. But the first effect is the one you want, not the second.[12]

---

[12] For a discussion and defence of this principle, see Nigel Biggar, *Aiming to Kill: The Ethics of Suicide and Euthanasia* (London: DLT, 2004), ch. 3.

What about abortion when the pregnancy was a result of a man committing rape?

In a justly famous essay, feminist philosopher Judith Jarvis Thompson argued that even if an embryo has a right to life, that doesn't necessarily make abortion wrong. She asks you to imagine that you have been kidnapped by the fictitious Society of Music Lovers and your circulatory system has been plugged into that of a sick violinist who needs kidney dialysis and whose life the Society wishes to save. He has a rare blood type, which you match, and he needs this dialysis for nine months. After that time, he will recover and you can be separated.

Are you morally obliged to stay plugged into him? The violinist has a right to life. But his right to life does not give the Society of Music Lovers the right to kidnap you and plug your system into his. It would be very kind of you to stay plugged in and save the musician's life. But nobody would regard it as murder if you insisted that the Society of Music Lovers set you free.

Jarvis Thompson's view is therefore that even if embryos are persons, women are not obliged to continue with any given pregnancy. As well as the embryo's right to life, the woman has a right to choose what happens to her body. Jarvis Thompson therefore argues that the woman's right to choose what happens to her body outweighs the embryo's right to life.

Jarvis Thompson's case does not work for abortion in general, because the discovery by a woman that she is pregnant does not come out of nowhere, as does the kidnap of the person by the Society of Music Lovers in her scenario. Ordinarily, the mother and her sexual partner have *already* made a choice which they knew could result in the conception of a child. Their choices led to the creation of this new life, and they are therefore responsible for its wellbeing. (Hence, the father of a child is quite rightly meant to contribute to the child's maintenance, even if he doesn't 'want' to have the child.) This is different to the scenario with the violinist, because the kidnap victim did not cause the violinist's condition.

But the kidnap scenario does provide an analogy to conception which has taken place as a result of rape. Unlike a pregnancy resulting from consensual sex, the woman in no sense chose the pregnancy. Of course, some women at this point do continue with the pregnancy, a course of action which can be humbling and beautiful, as well as, no doubt, challenging and painful.[13] But I find it hard to say that they are obliged to do so.

There is a second reason why I think that abortion of a pregnancy which results from rape could be legitimate. The pregnancy is the consequence

---

[13] For example, see the moving story of Heather Gemmen in *Startling Beauty: My Journey from Rape to Restoration* (Eastbourne: Kingsway, 2004).

of the original assault upon the mother. In a sense, it prolongs the violation which she has suffered.[14] Even worse, it might be said to perpetuate the connection to the man who raped her. In such circumstances, abortion is performed with the intention of ending the consequences of the rape – rather than intending to end the life of the child. We can apply the test which we used earlier to show that abortion to save the life of the mother is legitimate: if the baby somehow miraculously survived, and was adopted by another family, the mother would still have achieved her goal of no longer being pregnant as a result of the violation she suffered. She has nothing directly against the child, as it were, and her goal is not to end its life, but to stop the consequences of the violation she has suffered.

We need to make an important qualification here. We must not expect that abortion in such a case will somehow turn back the clock to before

---

[14] Although some women feel that having an abortion would *increase* the violation. This is the view of Jennifer Christie, who was raped by a man and chose to go ahead with the resulting pregnancy. See 'Raped While on a Business Trip, My Husband and I Chose Life', December 2014, online at http://savethe1.blogspot.co.uk/2014/12/raped-while-on-business-trip-my-husband.html. The whole site includes many beautiful and moving stories which show that God redeems even this awful circumstance.

the rape. As Jonathan Jeffes puts it, abortion is not a time machine. It cannot change the fact that a pregnancy took place, and that if nothing had been done, a child would have been born. Whilst the prospect of continuing with the pregnancy could be extremely troubling for the woman, it is important to recognise that abortion often causes its own problems. Many women who have had abortions experience post-abortion stress, so it is possible that the abortion will brings its own negative consequences for the woman.

One further striking point is that abortion following rape is by no means automatic. In one American study, 50 per cent of women chose to have an abortion following rape, 32 per cent opted to keep their child, 6 per cent went through with the pregnancy and put the child up for adoption, and 12 per cent had miscarriages.[15] And research has found that the majority of women who choose to keep the child are glad they did. I am by no means advocating that abortion is necessarily the best or only option following rape. But I do think that it is a legitimate option for them in the circumstances.

Conclusion

I have covered some very difficult ground here, and I've tried to do so sensitively. It has not been

---

[15] See the information at http://www.ncbi.nlm.nih .gov/pubmed/8765248.

possible to address everything, and if you are looking for further guidance on the emotional and pastoral side of abortion, I've listed more information in the Go Deeper section below. For now, I'm going to set out my conclusions, based on the biblical perspective which I set out earlier.

First, Scripture prohibits the destruction of innocent life, especially its deliberate destruction.

Second, it does so because humans are made in God's image and are precious to God.

Third, what makes us human is not whether we are rational, sentient or conscious, but whether we are physically alive. This means that life begins at the moment at which it begins physically, that is, conception (fertilisation). Several passages in the Bible corroborate this by indicating that God is intimately involved in and concerned with human life from a very early stage of its development in the womb. Some verses even refer explicitly to conception as the point at which a new human life begins. So, it is usually deeply wrong to deliberately destroy human life after conception has taken place.

Fourth, because the destruction of innocent human life is so tragic and evil, even if you are not convinced that human life begins at conception, you are obliged to treat it *as if* it begins at conception, unless you can prove otherwise beyond all reasonable doubt.

This biblical and theological approach would rule out abortion simply because the pregnancy is unwanted (except when the child was conceived as a result of rape). A woman absolutely has the 'right to choose' whether to have a child or not. But that right to choose should be exercised before a man and a woman bring a child into existence. Even when contraception is properly used, sexual intercourse almost always carries with it the possibility of conception. When people sleep together, they know that it could result in a pregnancy. This also partly explains why rape is a possible exception to this, because the woman has had no say in the pregnancy until after conception. Whilst we must beware of assuming that abortion is in her best interests after rape, it seems to me that it is at least a decision which she must make.

This approach also rules out abortion because the child will be disabled, tests such as amniocentesis which carry a risk and no medical benefit to the child, the destruction of 'surplus' embryos created through IVF and their use in scientific experimentation, and forms of so-called contraception which function not by preventing conception, but by inhibiting implantation (i.e. most intrauterine devices and some forms of the pill).[16]

A more ambiguous area is emergency contraception, especially the so-called morning-after pill. The best available evidence is that it prevents ovulation, but that it does not prevent an embryo from implanting once fertilisation has

---

[16] See *The Only Way is Ethics: Hoping for Children.*

already taken place (whereas intrauterine devices certainly inhibit implantation as well as fertilisation). However, because the pill may decrease the thickness in the endometrial lining of the womb, some people fear that it might lessen the chance of an embryo implanting. This seems less likely to me, because when the morning-after pill is taken too late to prevent ovulation, the resulting rate of pregnancy is much the same as it would be otherwise, suggesting that the pill does not hinder implantation.[17]

What should we do?

Abortion takes place in our society on a vast scale and directly affects a third of women, and therefore many men too. It is incredibly unlikely that the laws governing abortion will change any time soon and, even if they were to change the abortion pill (RU 146) would still be readily available by post over the internet. Just as we look back on the era before the abolition of slavery or on Nazi Germany and wonder how entire societies could collude with situations which are so self-evidently

---

[17] See the review of research in 'Emergency Contraception: A Last Chance to Prevent Unintended Pregnancy' by James Trussell, Elizabeth G. Raymond, and Kelly Cleland, online at http://ec.princeton.edu/questions/EC-Review.pdf, especially pages 5–7 on 'Mechanism of Action'.

wrong, no doubt one day others will look back and wonder at our stupor.

We must remember that this is a situation with which our entire culture colludes, because only that will prevent us from demonising vulnerable women in crisis pregnancies. Far from being offered a genuine 'right to choose', they have never been presented with the facts about contraceptive failure before they become pregnant and are offered no realistic alternative to abortion after they become pregnant. Yet Christians and the church could make a big difference by adopting some very simple steps:

1. Develop an informed approach to unintended pregnancy in your own life and for the lives of those around you. Consider what you would do if you or your spouse or partner became pregnant unintentionally. If you are a parent, minister or youth leader, discuss contraception and contraceptive failure, especially with young people and young adults.

2. Break the silence. Talk about abortion sensitively but openly. Don't treat it as something secret and shameful, but as a common part of life today. Women and men who have experienced past abortions need safe places in which they can process what has happened and find healing and hope.

3. Do everything you can to welcome and support women who get pregnant outside marriage. Don't let your family or church be a place where the subliminal message is, 'Don't you dare show up here pregnant.' People who go ahead with unintended

pregnancies make a costly and counter-cultural choice, and need our admiration and support.

I believe that, far from creating an atmosphere of judgement or condemnation, the biblical approach I have outlined here is the essential foundation for this kind of compassionate but informed response to abortion – and I pray that, for you, reading this is not the end of the process, but one step towards developing such a response for yourself.

Go Deeper

Jonathan Jeffes, *Abortion: Breaking the Silence in the Church* (Chichester: Lean Press, 2013).
Sarah Williams, *The Shaming of the Strong: The Challenge of an Unborn Life* (Eastbourne: Kingsway, 2005).
John Wyatt, *Matters of Life and Death: Human Dilemmas in the Light of Christian Faith* (Nottingham: IVP, 2009), chs 4 and 6–8.

Hoping for Children

The dilemmas of fertility treatment and adoption

The couple sat in my office. She was in tears. A well-meaning friend had given her a seeming prophecy that she was going to have a baby, despite the fact that their doctors said this was not going to happen naturally. Unless God did a miracle, they would need to use eggs donated by another woman to get pregnant.

As well as adding even more pressure and emotion to a situation that was already full of both, this possible prophecy complicated the decision-making process too. If God had said that they were going to get pregnant, were they lacking faith if they went ahead with fertility treatment? Or could such a treatment be God's way of giving them the child they longed for, using modern medical science to fulfil his purposes?

This is based on a true story – and one I have seen a number of times, with variations. One in seven couples experience fertility difficulties. I have spoken to many couples who have come to see me because they feel they have nobody else to talk to. In church, we tend not to discuss these intimate questions openly – although one recent development is a course for couples who are

'Waiting for Children', which offers them a much-needed guilt-free space to explore the issues, receive prayer and support, and hear from others with similar experiences.[1] They want to be faithful to God – and they desperately want children.

Here, I will start by looking at the theological reasons why it is natural and right for married couples to desire children. I will therefore argue that whilst adoption can and should be a wonderful and fulfilling vocation, fertility treatment is in principle also legitimate. However, I will suggest that marriage between a woman and a man is the right context for fertility treatment, and that it should not involve the exploitation or destruction of human embryos. I am aware that I can't cover all of the emotional and practical questions that arise, but I have found that helping people to develop an informed ethical perspective of their own also helps them practically and emotionally.

Is it selfish to want children in the first place?

In our culture, there can be a negative attitude to this deep desire to have children. Children are a

---

[1] For information about the course, see http://www.htb.org/whats-on/courses/waiting-children. There is also a very good article about the pain of infertility here: http://www.premierchristianity.com/Past-Issues/2013/April-2013/Just-the-Two-of-Us.

gift not a right, we are sometimes reminded. And couples unable to have children through natural means can adopt. This is quite true. But the *tone* underlying such comments can be negative, as if seeking children through fertility treatment is almost selfish.

Of course, it's possible to want children for the wrong reasons – to satisfy unmet needs for love, or to live vicariously through them. But the desire of a couple for a child of their own is not inherently selfish. It's a bit like marriage. When you marry someone, you think they will make you happy. But love is so much more than that. You also marry them because you want to make them happy.

The desire for children is a lot like that. Yes, children bring huge joy, fulfilment and fun (as well as stress and exhaustion)! Yes, children can make us happier and more fulfilled. But the reason why it is fulfilling to marry and have children is not selfishness, but precisely because we have been made by God to be loved by and to love other people. We are most fulfilled, not when we are wrapped up in ourselves but when we are caring for others and being loved by them. Having children is therefore both fulfilling *and* unselfish. (Not that marriage and parenthood are the only ways of being fulfilled, as I discuss in *Sexual Singleness*.)

We can go further. The desire for children is in fact given by God; it is part of the way God made us. In the creation story in Genesis 1, as soon as God creates women and men in his own image, he blesses them and tells them to be fruitful and increase. Although procreation is not the only way of being fruitful, it is specifically blessed and encouraged by God, and is therefore not inherently selfish. So given that this is how God has made us, no wonder most married couples want children of their own. Far from being selfish, it is natural and godly.

This is why, in the Bible, God shows such a concern and heart for those who cannot have children. Just occasionally, childlessness is portrayed as God's judgement on sin (for example, 2 Sam. 6:23). Misapplying verses like these causes great guilt for some people with fertility difficulties, who worry that they may have committed some sin for which God is punishing them. If you are in that situation, it is good to be reminded that infertility in the Bible is far more often portrayed as a tragedy, not a punishment. Far from being sent by God, it is a situation which God redeems and transforms (such as Sarah in Gen. 18, Hannah in 1 Sam. 1, and Elizabeth in Luke 1). So of course, the first thing a couple will do is to pray for God to intervene, in the confidence that they are asking a compassionate God to do something that he wants to do. But what if, after prayer, things do not change? What options are then right for that couple to explore?

Should couples with fertility difficulties adopt instead?

Having fertility difficulties does not automatically imply a calling to adopt. Adoption can be brilliant for couples who have thoughtfully and prayerfully decided that it is right for them. But adoption in the UK today very rarely means adopting a baby. Usually, older children need adopting, many of whom have complex emotional and behavioural needs. For these and other good reasons, some couples will decide that adoption is not right for them. Also, regarding adoption as a fall-back for couples who cannot have children naturally de-means adoption. It is not a fall-back option but a good calling in itself, although some couples discover their calling to adoption *through* their fertility difficulties. But it is not automatic.[2]

A less common option, but one worth consid-ering, is embryo donation or adoption. In the UK, this does not require a full legal adoption pro-cess, but is regarded as an act of donation from a couple who do not want or are unable to use the embryo in their own fertility treatment.[3] Whilst the child is not genetically that of the adopting

_____

[2] There is some great information about adop-tion from a Christian perspective at http://www.homeforgood.org.uk/.

[3] For information about embryo donation in the UK, see http://www.hfea.gov.uk/81.html and http://www.ngdt.co.uk/embryo-donor.

couple, this gives them the chance to bond with the child through pregnancy and birth, and to raise the child from infancy. Like adoption, taking in an existing embryo who would otherwise be discarded needs careful discernment. But morally I think it is a much better option than using donated sperm and/or eggs to *create* one, as I will explain below. Of course, this route will not be available to some couples, depending on the cause of their infertility.

Who should consider having fertility treatment?

As I have already said, procreation is blessed by God. It's important now to point out that it's not procreation in general which is blessed, but procreation *between wife and husband*. We see this at the end of Genesis 2: Adam and Eve are joined together by God into 'one flesh'. This is a reference to sex, to the physical joining of a man and woman who love one another so much that they want to be permanently united. One of the beautiful ways that God has made us is that it is precisely this intimate, loving physical union which has the potential to bring about a child. This child is the couple's own flesh and blood – he or she is a result of the parents' 'one flesh' union. Through the fusion of sperm and egg, the child is quite literally a physical union of their two bodily existences. Children therefore embody the love and delight that their parents have for one another.

So whilst the desire to have children is good and natural, so is the fact that procreation takes place through sex within marriage. It is no accident that children come into being through intimacy and passion for another person, by giving yourself bodily and receiving the gift of another's body in the context of a secure relationship in which they are then raised. Although an element of choice and decision is involved, children do not come into being through choice alone. They come into being through love.

So the desire for children is God-given. But the way to have children is also God-given. Children come through the love and security of sex within the committed relationship of marriage, because love and security are exactly what children need the most.

This leads me to believe that, in principle, Christians should welcome the idea of fertility treatment, although, like any medical treatment, nobody should feel obliged to have it. But provided the treatment itself is morally acceptable, married couples shouldn't feel guilty about treatments which seek to help their marriage to 'be fruitful' in the way that, in creation, God intended it to be.

However, whilst we should welcome fertility treatment in principle, at times we cannot welcome specific examples of it in practice, especially if it bypasses the God-given means of procreation, namely sexual union between wife and husband. I have said that the desire to have children is good. But that doesn't automatically mean we can use any and every means available to have them. It is in marriage and it is through sex that God intends procreation to take place. We should welcome fertility treatment, but not when it goes beyond the way God has made us.

For this reason, in the rest of this chapter I will be talking about fertility treatment for married opposite-sex couples. I do not think that single people or same-sex couples should use fertility treatments to create children for themselves outside opposite-sex marriage (I have explained in *QUILTBAG: Jesus and Sexuality* why I think marriage can only be between a woman and a man). Their desire to have children is totally understandable and legitimate, and of course they might well make fantastic parents. I see no objection at all to them adopting children, if they wish and if they are deemed suitable.[4] But adoption is different to bringing a child into the world in order to satisfy a desire to have children through a means other than sexual union within marriage.

---

[4] This is because, whilst it is usually in the child's best interests to be raised by their mother and father, children who need adopting are by definition already in a situation where they cannot be raised by their biological parents. It seems much better to me that those children should be in loving and secure single-parent or same-sex-parent families than in residential care. I'm well aware that not everyone will see it this way!

This is something that can cause guilt for people who have already taken this step, and even for children who have been born this way, who had no say in the matter. A biblical example which is helpful here is Hagar and Ishmael (see Gen. 16 and 21). Sarah and Abraham had been promised a child by God. But rather than waiting patiently for God to do what he had promised, Abraham sleeps with Sarah's servant, Hagar. This creates rivalry between Sarah and Hagar, which leads Sarah to be abusive towards Hagar. Seeking children outside marriage is shown to cause problems!

But whilst Hagar's son, Ishmael, was conceived in a way which God did not intend, that does not put God off him. God cares about and looks after both of them. Having children outside marriage should not stigmatise the child (in the way that children born as a result of extramarital sex used to be unjustly stigmatised).

Having set out some theological foundations for thinking through fertility treatment, we're now going to get down to some of the treatments couples might consider today, and think through the ethical issues which they raise.

Are there any fertility treatments which don't raise any moral problems?

Couples who experience difficulties conceiving (defined as trying unsuccessfully for more than a year) may first be expected to try simple measures such as improved diet and exercise, timing sex to coincide with ovulation, and so on. Of course, many couples will be doing this already. One myth to bust is that infertility relates to stress: 'Just relax and let it happen,' couples are sometimes told by well-meaning people. This is likely to increase the stress and pressure on them, and in any case the evidence does not suggest that stress necessarily inhibits conception and pregnancy.

The NHS estimates that for 25 per cent of couples, the cause of their fertility difficulties cannot be identified.[5] But receiving a diagnosis can be equally challenging – for example, one partner being the 'cause' of the infertility can obviously raise its own challenges – perhaps causing feelings of guilt or anger. Everybody is different, and it is crucial for couples to let themselves be themselves – they do not have to feel or respond a particular way.

If a diagnosis is made, treatment will be tailored accordingly. If the issue is, for example, a blockage in either the epididymis in the man's testicles or the woman's fallopian tubes, surgery holds no ethical problems. The same applies to womb transplants, in my view, although clearly they are a dramatic and invasive intervention which women will want to consider carefully before taking

---

[5] See http://www.nhs.uk/Conditions/Infertility/Pages/Causes.aspx.

the risk. In all these cases, medicine is simply trying to bring fallen human nature more into line with God's original intentions. The couple still conceives through sexual intercourse. The same could be said for drugs which aid or stimulate ovulation.[6] These interventions try to heal the body or encourage it to act in the way that it should, so that the couple can be naturally fruitful.

Is it OK to use artificial insemination, using the husband's sperm?

Intrauterine insemination (IUI) has a relatively low success rate but is usually much less invasive and costly than IVF, although men with a low or absent sperm count may need an operation to try to extract sperm directly. As Richard Higginson points out, masturbation for such a purpose (and similarly for the diagnosis stage, where men give a sperm sample for analysis) need not involve the husband masturbating on his own – the semen could be obtained through a 'loving sexual encounter' between husband and wife.[7]

---

[6] I mean only that these treatments are not *ethically* problematic. These drugs can have side-effects on some women, and therefore they will need to weigh up such factors carefully in deciding whether or not to take them.

[7] Richard Higginson, *Reply to Warnock* (Cambridge: Grove Books, 1986), p. 9.

IUI is not compatible with Roman Catholic teaching. Catholic teaching rules out forms of artificial contraception (such as condoms and the pill) because they separate sex from procreation. It therefore also rules out fertility treatments which do the same thing.[8] This view takes very seriously the point that God has not only given us the desire to procreate, but also the means of sexual intercourse within marriage. Sex and procreation are deliberately joined together by God for good reason and, to paraphrase Jesus's words from a different context, that which God has joined together, nobody should separate (Mark 10:9).

This view should not be dismissed carelessly. However, Protestants have on the whole considered contraception acceptable. We agree that sex and procreation are intrinsically connected. But we emphasise that sex is also about wife and husband joyfully and intimately expressing their mutual love, as well as about procreation. Of course, Catholic teaching agrees that love and joy are important within sex too! But Protestants

---

[8] The official Catholic teaching can be found in two documents: *Donum Vitae* (1987), online at http://www.vatican.va/roman_curia/congregations/cfaith/documents/rc_con_cfaith_doc_19870222_respect-for-human-life_en.html. And the more recent *Dignitas Personae* (2008), online at http://www.vatican.va/roman_curia/congregations/cfaith/documents/rc_con_cfaith_doc_20081208_dignitas-personae_en.html.

have tended to add that, because God does not intend every sexual act to be fruitful for procreation, procreation and sex can legitimately be separated – hence contraception is acceptable. As Martin Luther pointed out, the menstrual cycle, pregnancy and the menopause all entail seasons in which the couple is naturally infertile. In such times, sex may continue, but it is only able to fulfil one of its purposes. This does not undermine its goodness.

So, love and procreation are obviously connected by sex, but on the whole, Protestants have not thought that both purposes of sex have to be equally intended every time the couple make love. Sometimes the couple are particularly focussed on 'making' a baby. Usually, they will make love simply out of desire for and delight in one another. Procreation and sexual intimacy can therefore, to a certain extent, be separated.

Let's apply this to artificial insemination. In artificial insemination by husband (AIH), conception does not take place through sexual intercourse. Here, there is a separation of sex and procreation. But in my view it is a similar separation to the one involved in contraception. When using contraception, you intend sex without procreation. In AIH, you intend procreation without sex, although the sperm could have been obtained within the context of sexual intimacy. But the point is still to enable the husband and wife to conceive and be fruitful in the way that God intended them to be;

it is still procreation between husband and wife. I therefore think it is also a 'no problem' treatment.

Is it OK to use artificial insemination by donor (AID), donated gametes, or surrogacy?

Drawing on what I have just said, I do think that the involvement of third parties in fertility treatment is a problem. Third parties can be involved in a number of ways. Donor sperm may be used for artificial insemination by donor (AID), or for *in vitro* fertilisation (IVF, which we will discuss in the next section). IVF using donor sperm could use the eggs of the woman who will raise the child, or donated eggs. Equally, donor eggs could be combined with the sperm of the man who will raise the child. IVF can also take place using donor or intended parent gametes (sperm and eggs) with the resulting embryos implanted in a surrogate mother (for example if the intended mother has a condition which prevents implantation).

The phrase I have just used, 'intended parents' is rather awkward. Why not just say mother or father? Well, this is because a child could, in a sense, have as many as five 'parents': surrogate mother, egg donor, sperm donor, and rearing mother and father. Having quite that many would be unusual. But it's common enough for a child to have three or occasionally four 'parents' – the mum and dad who raise him or her, and a sperm or egg donor or surrogate. (There is also the possibility of transplanting the nucleus of one egg into another, when the mitochondrial DNA of an egg is faulty. Once fertilised, the embryo retains the healthy mitochondrial DNA and in a sense therefore has DNA from three rather than two people, although the mitochondrial DNA does not affect any of their phenotypical traits.[9])

The key question with respect to gamete donation and surrogacy is: what is going on here? Let's explore three possible analogies.

1) Is it like someone donating blood or, more dramatically, a kidney – the act of a Good Samaritan? The donor has more than they need, and the recipient has less. If so, the donor is genuinely a donor, not a parent. They go through robust counselling and a lengthy process which ensures that they understand that they will play their part and then walk away. But one difference is that organ and blood donations are matters of enabling someone to live a healthy life as God intended. They are about healing. Although infertility is a medical condition, childlessness is not. So donation and surrogacy are different to the 'no problem' treatments which work by healing. Here, medicine has become about *fulfilling*

---

[9] The technique and some of the ethical issues are discussed in '"Three-Parent Babies" Cure for Illness Raises Ethical Fear' by Ian Sample in *The Guardian*, 5 June 2012, online at: http://www.theguardian.com/science/2012/jun/05/mitochondrial-genetic-disease-ethical-doubts.

someone's desires, rather than *healing* their body. (Of course, many people will feel as if having a child in this way is tremendously healing in other respects.)

2) Donation and surrogacy could instead be compared to adoption and step-parenting, where a child is raised by one or more non-genetic parent. We normally regard that as a very good thing. But in an important way it is not like adoption. Adoption is about placing an existing child, whose parents are unable to raise it, with parents who can, whereas using donated gametes involves bringing a child into the world who wasn't there before.

3) A friend of mine, who chose not to use donor sperm, regarded it as more like adultery. This is extreme language, so let me explain her reasoning. If her husband had been severely injured and was no longer able to have sex at all, that would not make it right for her to seek a new sexual partner to fulfil her legitimate sexual desires – even if her husband was content for her to do so. She felt that her marital vow, 'for better, for worse' meant that if they were to have children, they should have them together or not at all. (They adopted, and later, much to their surprise, conceived naturally.)

Using donated sperm or eggs is clearly not equivalent to adultery, in the sense of deliberate sexual unfaithfulness. But my friend was onto something, namely that her marriage was something special as a union of two people into which it was not right to introduce a third party. The 'no problem' treatments above are 'no problem' precisely because they enable *the couple* to conceive as God intended. The problem with using donated gametes, and perhaps also surrogacy, is that these do not enable the couple to conceive. Yes, a child may be produced – but it is not simply their child, who has come into being as a result of their union with one another. (Not that they love one another or the child any less.) This is evident in the fact that, where donated sperm is used, masturbation has taken place which did not involve sexual intimacy between husband and wife. Medicine in this case does not enable the couple's marriage to be fruitful. Rather, it produces a child in order to satisfy their (entirely legitimate) desire for one.

From a Christian perspective, this is the most compelling reason not to use donated gametes, and similar questions might apply to surrogacy: it introduces a third party into the marriage, so that whilst it provides them with a child, it does not do so in a way which enables this particular couple to be fruitful as God intended.

There are some other, more general things to think about for people considering whether to use donated gametes or surrogacy. For example, in the UK, gamete donors cannot donate anonymously. When the child becomes 18, they have the right to find out who their genetic parents are, although only a small percentage of people take up this option. One couple who came to see me were considering using sperm from the husband's brother, so the child would be as genetically close as possible to their own child, and could have a close relationship with his or her genetic father as an uncle. They weren't sure whether to tell the child that his or her uncle was their genetic father in case this was confusing for the child – but, of course, the child could find out for themselves at 18.

Again, this tells us something about what is going on here. For the best of reasons, donors want to enable a couple to have children. But the act itself deliberately brings children into the world, at least one of whose genetic parents has already agreed not to be the person who raises them right from the word go. This is quite different to adoption, where a parent or parents have chosen to give up an existing child, or because the courts have decided that adoption is in the child's best interests. That is, adoption does not exist to provide children for infertile couples; it exists to provide parents for children who need them. It is a beautiful act in response to a situation of tragedy. But this itself shows that our preference is ordinarily for birth parents to raise their children, even though we know that in a fallen world it doesn't always work out that way. It seems odd, therefore, that we would deliberately create a child whom we already know will not be raised by one or both of his or her genetic parents. Put more bluntly, this shows that gamete donation exists to serve the interests of the parents, not the child.

This picks up our earlier point: who *are* the parents of the child? What makes someone a parent? This question is particularly acute when a dispute arises over who should raise the child (as in cases where a surrogate has borne the child and wants to 'keep' him or her, a kind of modern Solomon's choice).[10] But the questions are there even when there is no dispute: 'Whose' is the child? Who does the child 'belong' to? Who should 'keep' them?

I am not saying that, because these are tricky questions to answer, we should avoid using donated gametes. I am saying that the fact that we have to ask these questions reveals that a shift has taken place in the meaning of parenthood. It makes it harder to speak of the parents' relationship to the child without resorting to the language of ownership. There is something in the process which has made the child into a *product* made for particular people and who therefore somehow belongs to them, rather than a gift and responsibility which comes to parents. Of course, these parents still see the child as a gift – indeed, they may be all the more conscious of this because of what they have been through. But we have taken the step of treating the child as someone who

[10] See 1 Kings 3:16–28.

is there to satisfy their parents' desires, and the family being something which is there by parental design and choice. I'll return to this shortly.

Is it OK to have IVF and ICSI (intracytoplasmic sperm injection)?

I have claimed that IVF using donated gametes and surrogacy is something couples should avoid because it crosses a line by bringing in a third party into their marriage, and is not therefore about making their relationship fruitful. But most couples would prefer to use their own gametes anyway, if they can. In such cases, is IVF OK from a Christian perspective? (What I say here about IVF also applies to ICSI, where a single sperm is injected directly into an egg – a technique that may be used if the man has a very low sperm count.)

My answer is, 'Yes, in principle'. As with AIH, Roman Catholic teaching would not agree, because IVF and ICSI clearly go beyond the God-given means of conception through sexual intercourse. As with AIH, there is a separation of procreation from sex. But I think it is a morally acceptable separation, because the purpose of IVF is still to enable the couple to be naturally fruitful. So, yes, in principle. But IVF also raises some major questions which couples need to think through carefully beforehand.

The first question is that of the 'surplus' embryos that IVF may produce. If life begins at conception/fertilisation – as I have argued in *When Does Life Begin?* – there is no such thing as a 'surplus' embryo. They are all precious human lives, created in God's image. A woman who went through several rounds of IVF without a single viable embryo ever being produced once pointed this out to me in great anguish.

What I mean by 'surplus', then, is that a cycle of IVF can produce several embryos, whereas most parents these days tend to have two or three children, and judging by the reaction my wife and I received when we told people we were expecting our fourth child, very few people indeed want as many as four! If you believe that life begins at conception, it follows that all of those embryos should be given a chance at implantation. It is not likely that they will all successfully implant – but it is possible. So, the couple needs to think and talk this through very carefully *beforehand*, to pin down what they think about when human life begins and to 'count the cost' before they reach the point – perhaps not until many years later if they have the embryos frozen – when they must decide what to do with their remaining embryos. At this point, they have four options. They can seek to have more implanted (expensive and they may end up with a larger family than they want or can cope with). They can allow the embryos to be destroyed. They can allow them to be used in research. (Both of these options would be deeply wrong if you believe that they are human beings.) Or they can donate them to another couple, as discussed above (although there is no guarantee they will be used, in which case you may still need to decide between one of the first three options). It's obviously much better to make these decisions before treatment, rather than once the embryos exist.

An option that could be explored earlier on in the process is to ask the clinic only to fertilise a few eggs at a time or to have natural cycle IVF, which harvests only the mature egg that would have been released naturally in the woman's monthly cycle, rather than several eggs at once.[11] This will have a disproportionate impact on the woman, if she later has to endure additional operations to harvest eggs. (This is because, whilst eggs can be frozen, they consequently have a lower success rate.) And of course, it will be more expensive. I know couples who, having prayed about it, decided to go ahead with IVF, but committed to give each embryo the chance to be implanted. This is just the right *attitude* – but it's a high-risk *strategy*. On the whole, they ended up with two or three children. But one family ended

---

[11] It is also cheaper and does not require the use of fertility drugs – but it has a lower success rate than conventional IVF. Some basic information is available on the HFEA website here: http://www. hfea.gov.uk/natural-cycle-ivf.html.

up with more children than they felt they could cope with. They believed (as do I) that seeking to implant all the embryos wasn't a case of having more children, but of nurturing and loving the children they had already chosen to have. The point is, it's unpredictable. If life begins at conception, the fact that you don't know for sure how many embryos you will get means that you don't how many children you will get. You cannot control the outcome.

Whilst many people participate in IVF with great caution and responsibility, for those who believe that human life begins at conception there can be no doubt that IVF as a whole has resulted in the deliberate destruction of countless lives, many as involuntary human victims of scientific experimentation. Therefore, some Christians choose not to have IVF, even if they do not think it is wrong in principle, because they believe that the way in which it is practised makes it institutionally or structurally sinful. They do not want to participate in this system, particularly because many of the scientific gains on which IVF is based today have been made on the basis of research on (and therefore destruction of) 'surplus' embryos.

I find this a very compelling concern. At an early point in our marriage, my wife was diagnosed with polycystic ovaries. This can make it harder for some couples to conceive, although in our case in the end it did not prevent us from conceiving naturally. When we were coming to terms with the diagnosis, we decided that we would not want to have IVF if that option was offered to us. But I can see why others legitimately choose to have IVF, provided they guard against experimentation on or destruction of their embryos.

Related to this are the questions of freezing and screening embryos. Freezing puts some people off IVF, because there have been fears that the freezing and thawing process may be harmful to the embryos. However, research so far has not found evidence of this. Screening to assess which embryos are the healthiest and most viable is more problematic, because it implies that only the healthiest embryos will be used and the rest discarded. This can also be combined with pre-implantation genetic diagnosis (PGD), in which the genetic codes of the embryos are analysed, to see if they will develop a genetic disease such as cystic fibrosis or sickle-cell anaemia. This may seem like an amazing advance, as it enables parents who have such diseases or who are genetic carriers of them to ensure they will not give birth to children with these debilitating and often terminal conditions. However (to return to this point once again), if life begins at conception then it cannot be right to discard an embryo simply because it will develop such a disease. Discriminating against particular human beings just because they are sick or disabled is deeply wrong, and indeed is illegal in almost any other circumstance, and rightly so.

Finally, and very practically, the couple need to be aware of the emotional and physical roller-coaster which IVF sets them on, especially the prospective mother. Whilst this is true of all fertility treatments (and indeed of natural conception!), it is particularly true of IVF. As well as the operation to harvest the eggs, the many injections, scans, and hormone drugs all take their toll. And the success rate of any given cycle of IVF is about 25 per cent. So, as well as the ethical issues to consider, the couple should consider carefully how much they want and are able to invest (emotionally, in time, and financially). No treatment guarantees results, and all treatments are costly in more ways than one. Many couples find it hard but manageable to have some cycles of IVF, even if they are unsuccessful. But if conception continues to prove elusive, it may ultimately be helpful (though undeniably painful) to set a limit.

Couples who experience fertility difficulties are more likely to break up than those who do not, so investing in their relationship, enjoying one another's company, having sex for intimacy and not just conception, and having fun together is absolutely crucial. It is natural and right for couples to focus strongly on pursuing conception for a time if they want to, but few couples can sustain this kind of pressure indefinitely.

So, is it right to have IVF? I have answered yes, in principle, when IVF plays the role of helping a couple to be fruitful as God intended. But there are possibilities within IVF which a couple should not choose. If a couple discards embryos once they have the desired number of children, screens them so they only use the healthiest, or involves a third party, this suggests that the process has become a matter of getting what they want, rather than seeking to be fruitful and accepting the children who come their way, with all the risks and uncertainties which that involves.

Commercialisation

In the UK, there has rightly been resistance to some aspects of the commercialisation of fertility treatment. For example, it is not legal to pay somebody for their gametes, for acting as a surrogate, or for donating an embryo. At the time of writing, they are entitled to receive £35 for expenses. But whilst the donor cannot profit from their donation, other people do. For example, the London Sperm Bank charges people who want to receive a sperm donation £950. And the fact that fertility treatment can and often is provided on a private health basis means that the treatment itself can be highly commercialised. First, this means that treatment is more readily available to those who can afford it. It is the prerogative of the wealthy. Second, advertising may make use of highly emotive images of happy babies with their parents. This is exploitative and manipulative of vulnerable people. Third, clinics understandably promote themselves on the basis of their success rate in helping couples achieve pregnancy and, therefore, on the basis that they provide value for money, which provides them with a disincentive not to provide treatments which are less likely to succeed (such as natural cycle IVF or cycles which harvest a smaller number of eggs due to concerns about creating surplus embryos). Fourth, when somebody is paying a substantial sum of money, it's only natural that they expect as high a quality 'product' as possible, which may mean sourcing and advertising the best possible sperm, or only implanting the healthiest embryos, which makes it more likely that weaker or less healthy embryos will be discarded. Fifth, although clinics cannot pay women for their eggs, some offer free IVF treatment to women who cannot afford it in return for egg donations, so an element of quid pro quo can be present, even if it is not a directly financial one.[12]

Whilst I do not believe that the commercialisation of fertility treatment makes such treatment wrong as such, I do believe it is a worrying development that will lead to children increasingly being seen as a product. This ties in to and exacerbates overly aspirational or 'pushy'

---

[12] For example, see this page from the website of the Lister Clinic: http://www.ivf.org.uk/faqs.

approaches to parenting – as in the notorious advert for the London Sperm Bank which invited people to 'Find Your Perfect Match' under cartoon pictures of doctors, teachers, accountants, actors and models!

Conclusion

The desire of a husband and wife to have a child of their own is godly and natural. Parenthood is fulfilling, but not selfish. Adoption (including adopting embryos) may be the right option for some – but infertility does not automatically entail a vocation to adoption. This must be discerned separately.

Children are 'begotten, not made'.[13] The more we step away from seeing children as the natural fruit of sexual union between a woman and a man who have committed their lives to one another, the more we tend to see them as products. If so, no wonder an element of 'quality' control creeps in through screening and post-implantation genetic diagnosis. So, whilst fertility treatment should be welcomed in principle, there are reasons to be concerned about the illusion of control

---

[13] This phrase, from the Nicene Creed, makes the point that Jesus is the Son of God the Father and therefore equal to him, not created by God and therefore at God's disposal. See Oliver O'Donovan, *Begotten or Made?* (Oxford: Oxford University Press, 1984).

over something that is meant to be about intimacy and self-giving.

I have given particular reasons why I do not regard surrogacy and the use of donated gametes to be ethically acceptable, although I do so in fear and trembling, knowing that for some couples this may close down the few treatment options which are open to them. By involving a third party in their marriage, this makes conception about the desire to *produce* a child *for* the couple, rather than enabling *them* to be fruitfully united as God intended.

I have, however, been in favour of IVF and artificial insemination using the gametes of the wife and husband. Even here, great care needs to be taken not to be making a human being for our own ends. Within IVF, I have therefore suggested that the couple should not be willing to discard embryos once they have the children they want, or because an embryo is unhealthy. Couples who agree with this conclusion will therefore want to be especially careful in counting the cost and discussing options with their clinic before they go ahead with treatment.

Go Deeper

John S. Feinberg and Paul D. Feinberg, *Ethics for a Brave New World* (Wheaton, IL: Crossway, 2nd edn, 2010), chs 9–10.

Gilbert Meilaender, *Bioethics: A Primer for Christians* (Grand Rapids, MI: Eerdmans, 3rd edn, 2013), chs 2–3 and 5.

David VanDrunen, *Bioethics and the Christian Life: A Guide to Making Difficult Decisions* (Wheaton, IL: Crossway, 2009), chs 4–5.

John Wyatt, *Matters of Life and Death: Human Dilemmas in the Light of Christian Faith* (Nottingham: IVP, rev. edn, 2009), ch. 3.

All also available as ebooks.

Tricky Decisions at the End of Life

Euthanasia and assisted suicide

In *When Does Life Begin?* I looked at what makes us human and, therefore, at when human life begins (and, by implication, ends). I tried to show that all human life is equally and intrinsically precious, because we are all made in God's image. That is what makes human life worth preserving and protecting. Our preciousness is not dependent on our achievements or qualities. I also argued that in the Bible, human life is inherently physical and, therefore, what makes us human is not whether we possess certain traits such as consciousness, rationality, independence or the ability to make our own choices. What makes us human is being physically alive human beings, so *personal* human life begins at fertilisation, the moment when *physical* human life begins.

If I'm right about this, my take on assisted suicide and euthanasia isn't hard to guess! Deliberately ending somebody else's life, or helping them to end their own, can never be right. It may seem kind, but it cannot really be kind to deprive them of the life that God has given them and cares about. But this leaves a lot of questions. How can we live this out when we go through, or see others go through, unbearable suffering? Should medical treatment have limits? Are there times when Christians can make their peace with death or should we always pray for healing? In what follows, I will try to show that there is a difference between deliberately ending or hastening the end of someone's life, and taking steps, such as declining or withdrawing a particular treatment, which are likely to have that effect but which are taken for other good reasons.

Recap: What makes life precious and when does it end?

I'm not going to go into the full biblical and theological detail about this here – for that, see the sections in *When Does Life Begin?* But I will provide a brief summary of my argument there, and apply it to the issue of euthanasia.

Human beings are created in God's image (Gen. 1:27). This is why human life is *always* precious: every human being is made in the image of God, regardless of their circumstances. Because our value comes from being like God, we cannot lose it by being incapacitated, or sick, or in pain. We are *intrinsically* precious, just by being who we are. We don't need to earn it or qualify for it. This is the *reason* that the Bible prohibits the deliberate taking of innocent human life (Gen. 9:6).

So, what makes us precious is the fact that we are human. But what makes us human? According to Scripture, it's not our so-called 'higher' abilities such as thinking, feeling, or the ability to make decisions. Rather, God has primarily made us physical, bodily creatures, out of the 'dust from the ground' (Gen. 2:7). Our bodies are good gifts! If we try to pinpoint some other quality as being the thing that really makes us human, such as our ability to speak and communicate, then that ability becomes the thing which we really value, rather than the human beings who possess it. The effect of this would be to exclude some human beings who are physically alive from being people whom we are called to care for and protect.

So, humans are intrinsically precious, and what makes us human is our human bodily life. This means that, just as we cannot pinpoint a time after the beginning of human bodily life at which we suddenly 'become' people who qualify for the usual protections and privileges of being human, we cannot say that we cease to be human any time before human bodily life ends. We are people from the time our lives begin physically until the time that they end physically.

Tricky decisions 1: Organ donation when someone has died

The Christian view about when life ends fits well with the current medical definition of death. In medical terms, the way that the end of life is currently defined is 'brain stem death' or 'whole brain death'. Someone in a persistent vegetative state (PVS), who has suffered the loss of their higher brain functions, is not considered medically dead. They may display sleep-awake patterns and other signs of consciousness, and they breathe naturally, whereas someone whose lower brain has also died will cease to breathe, and therefore will die in every other respect very shortly afterwards. It would be completely wrong, for example, to remove organs from someone in a PVS (that is, part of their brain has died), but it is routine (subject to consent) in the case of those whose entire brains have died.

This seemingly technical point is very important with respect to the donation of organs from those who have died. After a person whose organs are being donated has been pronounced brain dead, they are kept on an artificial respirator until the organs can be transplanted, because without oxygen the organs would quickly die too. Many family members feel a sense of comfort know-ing that although they have sadly lost their loved one, at least perhaps some good has come from the fact that some of their organs can be used to help other people who need and can use them. But others feel uncomfortable that organs are re-moved from their loved one whilst the deceased is seemingly still breathing. Are they really dead? And if they aren't dead, doesn't that mean that the removal of their vital organs will kill them?

This discomfort is understandable, but it is important to reassure people in this situation that their loved one is no longer physically alive. They should only be in this situation if they have genuinely already suffered from whole brain death, which would mean that the rest of their body would shut down immediately, if artificial ventilation was stopped. Of course, it would be a gross abuse of this definition to pronounce someone dead where death was merely imminent, simply in order to ensure that their organs could be used.

If somebody in excruciating pain wants to die, isn't it cruel that they should have to continue to live?

We must tread a fine line here. Intoxicated by the way in which God brings such wonderful salvation even out of the suffering of Jesus Christ, the Christian tradition has at times been too keen to affirm the value of suffering. Some Christians have even suggested that God *sends* it to test or improve us. This goes too far. In Scripture, the primary cause of suffering is the activity of the devil. It's true that some passages in the Old Testament give the impression that God allows suffering in order to test us (see Job 1 – 2 – although even here Satan clearly plays a major role). But by the New Testament, and especially in the teaching of Jesus, sickness and suffering are primarily attributed to Satan. For example, in Luke 13:16 it is Satan who has kept the woman bound, which is why healing the sick was such a key part of Jesus's mission, as he drove back the devil and established the Kingdom of God. In 1 John 3:8 it says, 'The reason the Son of God appeared was to destroy the works of the devil.' Of course, it's true that one consequence of the devil's activity is that humanity rebelled against God's goodness (Gen. 3:1–7), and God sent suffering and sickness as part of our punishment for that (Gen. 3:16–19). Sickness and suffering *in general* do come from sin and its punishment. But that doesn't mean that each *individual* person's suffering is a result of their individual sin. In fact, Jesus twice explicitly rejects this idea (Luke 13:1–5; John 9:1–3).

This has two implications. The first is that suffering, sickness and death were not God's original plan for the world. They are not consequences of being human, but of being fallen. God does not want things to be this way or for us to suffer. Indeed, death is an 'enemy' of God (1 Cor. 15:26). So, although God can certainly use and redeem suffering, that doesn't mean that God wants us to undergo it in the first place. Alleviating and avoiding suffering therefore makes sense and is a good and godly thing to do when it can be done legitimately. However, precisely because death is not what God wants, we should not try to bring it about ourselves. If death is an enemy of God, then God is opposed to it. We should not seek a truce with death by hastening it or seeking it out.

In Christ, God has defeated death – and it would be a betrayal of that victory to give in to it.

This leads to the second implication. We cannot escape suffering in our own strength – only God can liberate humanity and creation from the power of the devil and from our own sin. This should make us wary of the idea that we can evade pain and suffering by choosing the moment and the manner of our death. Alleviating pain and sickness is good, but we cannot escape or eradicate it in our own strength – least of all to eliminate suffering by eliminating the sufferer. Indeed, that would be idolatrous, taking God's role of reversing the Fall onto ourselves. So often (as, for example, in the case of communism), it is precisely the projects that claim the most for themselves in terms of establishing a new and radiant world order, which tend to bring about the greatest wrongdoing and human misery in their name. Death is an enemy – but Jesus has defeated it. We cannot and don't need to defeat it ourselves.

This attitude to death is beautifully expressed by St Paul at a time when he was himself suffering in prison. Like many in our society, Paul wanted to die: 'My desire is to depart and be with Christ, for that is far better' (Phil. 1:23). Because Jesus has defeated death, Paul does not fear it, but hopes for an end to his earthly suffering and the beginning of the eternal joy of full union with Christ. He therefore feels genuinely torn between life and death: 'Yet which I shall choose I cannot tell. I am hard pressed between the two' (vv. 22–23). This strengthens our sympathy and understanding for those whose suffering is so extreme that death *seems* preferable to life.

But that's not where Paul stops. It's true that 'to die is gain', but that does not lead him to undervalue life or to hasten death, because 'to live is Christ' (v. 21). Although it might be nicer for him to die and be united with Jesus, while Paul is alive he has work to do: 'If I am to live in the flesh, that means fruitful labour for me' (v. 22). His desire for his own peace and freedom from suffering is overcome by his desire to help the Philippians grow in their faith: 'to remain in the flesh is more necessary on your account' (v. 24). Therefore he concludes that 'I will remain and continue with you all, for your progress and joy in the faith' (v. 25). His focus is not on himself and his preferences, because he knows he exists not for himself but for the sake of others. He has a calling and purpose to fulfil – as do we all.

It might sound fine to say that a superstar Christian apostle like Paul can have a vocation and purpose even in the midst of suffering (which, as I hope is clear, is *not* the same as saying that God wants or sends the suffering). But someone who experiences suffering may not feel that way at all – nor may those close to them who have to watch them go through great pain. How can, for example, someone with motor neurone disease, who is becoming progressively locked-in and unable to move, have a vocation to still serve God? The very fact that this has become such a pressing question in our day shows precisely the kinds of traits we really value now: the ability to communicate, to act, to be independent. But, as we're about to see, the Christian idea of vocation is much richer than our ability to actually perform and achieve things.

If somebody wants to die, what right has anyone else to insist that they continue to live?

Dan James, who played rugby for the England Under-16s and hoped for a career as a profes-sional rugby player, was paralysed from the chest down after his spine was dislocated when a scrum collapsed during a rugby training session in March 2007. He committed suicide at the Dignitas flat in Zurich in September 2008 after travelling there with the assistance of his parents, who were questioned by the police for allegedly assisting him, but not prosecuted. (Nobody has been pro-secuted in the UK for accompanying someone to the Dignitas flat, and indeed a number of people from the UK have gone there to end their lives who were not even terminally ill.)

    Dan James's mother, Julie, wrote the following about his situation:

Dan found his life so unbearable and had tried to commit suicide three times . . . Whilst not everyone in Dan's situation would find it as unbearable as Dan, what right does any human being have to tell any other that they have to live such a life, filled with terror, discomfort and indignity, what right does one person who chooses to live with a particular illness or disability have to tell another that they should have to . . . Our son could not have been more loved and had he felt he could live his life this way he would have been loved just the same but this was his right as a human being, nobody but nobody should judge him or anyone else.[1]

This story is so moving, and we must begin with compassion and empathy towards people in such heart-rending situations that they are desperate to end their own lives swiftly and painlessly rather than endure an excruciating and drawn-out death, or in Dan's case to go on living with an utterly life-limiting condition. Julie James's eloquent comments highlight a major question in our culture today: is it compassionate to prevent people from helping others to end their lives? And is it a so-called 'imposition' of the views of one section of society on others? If so, the implication is that

---

[1] Julie James, 'Rugby Suicide: The Unedited Emails of His Mother' in *Daily Telegraph*, 18 October 2008, online at http://www.telegraph.co.uk/news/uknews/3219872/Rugby-suicide-the-unedited-emails-of-his-mother.html

it should be up to each individual to make the decision for themselves rather than for the law to govern the issue.

However, this way of thinking is not as neutral and impartial as it sounds. As we've seen, in our culture being human is essentially about being independent and free; humans are essentially separate. This way of thinking is suspicious of society, and tends to regard the views and claims of others as oppressing our freedom to do what we want. Individual choice is the highest value; someone has the right to decide what happens to their body, as if they are the only person with a claim to it. If you want to end your life, that's up to you. It is demeaning to be sick and humiliating to need others to care for you.

The antidote to this way of thinking is not judgement, but the much richer vision of what it is to be human offered to us by Scripture. Scripture shows us that humans have a deep need for one another. The biblical creation stories emphasise that human beings are communal and relational creatures. Genesis 1:27 notes that it is *together* that men and women are created in the image of God, and Genesis 2:18 reminds us that it is 'not good' for Adam to be alone. That is, we were never created for isolation: we *all* need one another. The sick, the severely disabled and the dying aren't just recipients of the care and love of others. They too have a calling and a purpose – something to offer others. Without them (both as a group and as individuals), human life would be vastly diminished. Not only is each of them intrinsically precious and made in the image of God, as we have seen, but they are each individually irreplaceable as someone's child, parent, friend, sibling, neighbour. They are called to be something to someone, and that personal and individual specialness is in no way diminished by their suffering, or terminal illness, or by not being physically or mentally well enough to communicate or act for themselves.

So, every suffering person has an individual and irreplaceable calling; each person is special and precious in themselves. But they also have a particular calling *because* of their condition, which comes to them through their condition. The healthy and the supposedly able *need* them. Why is this?

Anyone who has spent time caring for a sick or vulnerable person, such as a small child, a very sick parent, or a severely disabled person, will know that such an experience is deeply humbling. Caring for another does not make you feel superior to the vulnerable person! Rather, as we have seen, being vulnerable and needy is something which is intrinsic to being human. It is not a failing.

This is explored beautifully by Henri Nouwen in his memoir of being a carer for Adam, a severely disabled man. When he first met Adam, Nouwen says that 'in a flash I knew in my heart that this

very disabled human being was loved by God
. . . and sent into the world with a unique mission
of healing.'[2] What was this mission of healing –
how did such a severely disabled person offer
healing to such a capable and gifted person as
Henri Nouwen? Nouwen explains that 'washing,
feeding, and just sitting with Adam, gave me
the home I had been yearning for.'[3] In this way,
Adam became a holy person for Nouwen. Adam
became the person who 'more than any book or
professor led me to the person of Jesus.'[4]

Therefore, being brought face-to-face unavoid-
ably with the need and dependence of another
upon you, confronts you with your own vulnerability and need. Caring for the vulnerable helps
you glimpse your own humanity more clearly because, as we've seen, being human is not about
independence and freedom, but about interde-
pendence and relationship.

This is not to romanticise or idealise such conditions – anyone who has had a caring role will be
all too aware that there is nothing romantic about
intimate physical care for another person. And
Nouwen reflects this in his book: 'I didn't soften
or sweeten it.'[5] But it is, nonetheless, a privilege
from which the carer can receive insight and com-

---

[2] Henri J M Nouwen, *Adam: God's Beloved*
(Maryknoll, NY: Orbis, 1997), p. 15.
[3] *Adam*, p. 127.
[4] *Adam*, p. 16.
[5] *Adam*, p. 126.

munity – if they have ears to hear. Being needy does not eradicate one's humanity – it fulfils it. We all need the care of others – it's just that some of us are better at disguising this fact than others. Caring for someone helps us take off our own masks and admit our own needs.

This is why the vulnerability and absolute dependence of an embryo upon its mother, or a comatose or locked-in person on their carers, must not disqualify them from being protected and cherished as much as any other human life. Indeed, quite the opposite: the more vulnerable and fragile somebody is, the more concerned we should be to care for and help them, if we are to be people shaped by the compassionate heart of God for the vulnerable.

This leads to another and much more practical reason to be concerned about the suicide of someone like Dan James. He ended his life eighteen months after the horrific accident that paralysed him so severely. It seems unlikely that that is enough time for someone to come to terms with such a traumatic and life-changing catastrophe and to therefore reach a truly settled and objective decision that their life is no longer and never could be worth living. Indeed, if someone really does feel that way, then it's something of an indictment of our culture that our instinct is to assist them to end their lives, rather than to do whatever we can to help them feel differently, e.g. by offering much better care and support to

Dan and his family, counselling to help him process the enormous impact of his accident and the huge emotional upheaval it has wrought, and practical help to ensure that his life is genuinely stimulating and worthwhile.

Compare Julie James's words, for example, with those of Gillian Gerhardi, who suffered from cerebral palsy and then developed multiple sclerosis, a terminal illness.

> Every day, for three months, I plotted to kill myself. I was going to ride my motorised wheelchair down on to the high road and into the path of a lorry. But by obtaining a full-time care assistant funded by social services, and by re-casting my life to see beyond my useless body, I came through that dark time. I paint, I run a disabled theatre company, I live a full life.[6]

During her 'dark time', Gillian Gerhardi had a settled desire to end her life. What if she and many others like her had had the opportunity to end their lives before they came through their 'dark time'? Many people consider suicide at some point in their lives, and it is especially understandable that someone would do so after a tragic accident or if they were terminally ill. But

---

[6] Quoted in David Cohen, 'A £45 suicide in a Zurich flat – where's the dignity in that?' in the *Evening Standard* 26 January 2006. A copy of the article is online at http://www.willtolive.co.uk/pdf/20060126_a_45_suicide_in_a_zurich_flat.pdf.

normally when someone is considering suicide, we recognise that, far from helping them to do so, the right response is to offer them more support and care, to protect them from themselves and to help them come through that time. The fact that someone finds their life unbearable and is seriously committed to ending their lives is usually considered as a sign in itself that they need extra protection and support put in place precisely to help them come through this time if at all possible. It is extremely strange that we treat suicide in such circumstances as a tragedy which we have a duty to avert if at all possible, yet in other circumstances it is increasingly becoming seen as a right. In both cases, people may find their lives unbearable.

Should we always pray for healing (or resurrection) to take place?

Many Christians feel conflicted when it comes to praying for the terminally ill or those in extreme suffering. Should they keep praying for a miracle right up until the last minute – and then, after death, keep praying for resurrection? Others have sometimes felt that the kindest thing for someone in unremitting agony is to pray that God would 'take them' soon – perhaps even describing this as a sort of 'healing' in itself. Which is right?

When it comes to prayer, thankfully the whole point is that we are addressing our petitions to God – and it's up to God what to do with them! Personally, I don't think God does act to 'take quickly' people who are in unbearable pain – if God acts directly in the situation, surely it would be to heal rather than to kill – but, in any case, there's a big difference between praying for it, and acting to make it happen!

When it comes to praying for resurrection, I wonder if you've ever noticed that nearly all of the people raised from the dead by the Old Testament prophets and by Jesus and his apostles died in an untimely way. Elijah and Elisha pray for two children to be raised (1 Kings 17:21 and 2 Kings 4:35), Jesus raised the son of the widow of Nain who is described as a 'young man' (Luke 7:14), as is Eutychus, raised by Paul in Acts 20:9. Jairus's daughter is described as a 'little girl' in Mark 5:41 and as being 'about twelve' years old in Luke 8:42. We are not told how old Dorcas (Acts 9:36–43) and Lazarus (John 11) are.

I'm not saying that we shouldn't be bothered when the elderly die! As we've seen, every person is precious and their death is a genuine loss which God did not intend. But there is a strand within Scripture which recognises that dying when you are 'old and full of days', surrounded by your loved ones and looking back on a life of faithful service to God, has a certain rightness and peace about it. For example, the death of

Job is *not* regarded as part of his suffering (Job 42:17). We are meant to live forever – but not yet! As Psalm 90 puts it, 'The years of our life are seventy, or even by reason of strength eighty' (verse 10). This explains why, when a young life is cut off prematurely – say, the parent of a young child, or the death of a child before their parents – it seems intrinsically more tragic and unjust.

At the same time, we should not hold back from praying for the sick to be healed! Many Christians um and ah about whether healing in a particular case may or may not be 'God's will'. What this forgets is that Jesus, who is the fullest revelation of God, was always disposed to heal the sick – although as Mary and Martha, the sisters of Lazarus discovered, he doesn't always do so immediately. We must never, therefore, think that God wants someone to be sick in order to punish them, for example, or because he wants them to learn some particular lesson. We see in the cross of Christ that God is present in sickness and suffering, and we see in Jesus's resurrection that he redeems and brings good out of suffering. But that doesn't ever mean that he *wants* it in the first place. Sickness is not God's will. Rather, we see in Christ that God's will is to restore creation to the way God always wanted it to be.

So, we can and should always pray for the sick to be healed, secure in the knowledge that we are praying in accordance with God's will. We should not do so aggressively – and sometimes it may be most sensitive to pray privately rather than in front of someone who is dying and their loved ones. But we can *ask* – it's up to God to answer!

Yet, as we all know only too well, not all sickness is miraculously healed. This was true in the New Testament too. Sometimes Jesus's own disciples prayed and did not see healing (see Mark 9:18). No doubt many people were praying for healing for Epaphroditus, but he didn't recover until he had been so sick that he almost died (Phil. 2:27). Presumably Paul prayed for Timothy's stomach trouble to be healed – but he also recommended that he drink some wine to help too (1 Tim. 5:23). Even Jesus, occasionally, was prevented from doing 'many' miracles by the unbelief of those around him (Mark 6:5–6). Plenty of Christians died in New Testament times and were not raised from the dead – although death became seen as much less significant, so that Paul often followed the example of Jesus by referring to death as being asleep (1 Thess. 4:13). Even Jesus's own miracles were in a sense limited. He fed the 5,000; they got hungry again. He raised Lazarus from the dead – and presumably, later on, Lazarus had the dubious distinction of being one of the few people in history to die for a second time!

So, on the one hand, Jesus brought the kingdom of God and therefore he healed the sick. Jesus showed us definitively that God does not want sickness and indeed is actively working to prevent human suffering. In his cross and re-surrection, Jesus has utterly defeated sickness, suffering and death. I warned earlier that death cannot be avoided and that we should resist pro-jects which try to overcome all suffering. But the fact that Jesus healed the sick and opposed suf-fering obviously means that alleviating suffering is kingdom work, not an arrogant rejection of human fallenness. Medicine has a real Christian vocation and authorisation. Healing the sick is part of the ministry which Jesus gives to his disciples. It is a sign that God's kingdom really has come.

But, on the other hand, whilst we are waiting for Jesus to come back again, the kingdom of God is not yet fully here. We don't yet always experi-ence the full benefits of Jesus's victory. As we've seen, we need to be suspicious of triumphalism in prayer or in medicine which assumes that sick-ness and even death can and must *always* be evaded, because only God can bring in the king-dom fully. We can alleviate sickness and suffering, but we cannot always overcome them. This lays the foundation for answering our next question too.

Tricky decisions 2: Are there times when we should decline treatment, or let people go and allow death to follow naturally?

Earlier, I showed that we must never deliberately take the life of another person or help them to take their own life, because each individual is precious to God. The fact that they may be experiencing severe suffering or be in, say, a vegetative or locked-in condition in no way diminishes that. In short, I think it is wrong to end someone's life simply because of our human assessment of their 'quality of life'.

However, I believe that there is a difference between deliberately ending one's life and declining a potentially life-prolonging treatment. For example, a patient with terminal cancer might decide not to undergo yet another round of chemotherapy. We wouldn't describe this as suicide! Similarly, their doctor might decide that such a treatment is not in their best interests. This does not mean that he or she is deliberately trying to end their life.

So, what is the difference between deliberately ending a life and declining a treatment? It can't simply be that in one case you act and in the other case you refrain from acting. Sometimes it would be seriously wrong to refrain from acting – for example, if you see somebody in a life-threatening situation, such as a non-swimmer falling overboard from a ship or a young child playing on a road. The outcome in both cases is the same: death comes sooner than it might otherwise have done. So, what is the difference here?

The difference is that, sadly, the patient is beyond medical power to *cure*. They're in a genuinely different situation to, for example, a child playing in the road. If a patient was genuinely curable, it really *would* be wrong to refuse to treat them. But I'm talking here only about treatments which might *prolong* someone's life a little while longer, rather than make them better.

An important consideration for patients, doctors and loved ones in these circumstances is that life-prolonging treatments very often can diminish the quality of their remaining life. I've said that I don't think poor quality of life is a legitimate reason to end someone's life deliberately. But that's quite different to deciding whether or not someone who is *already* dying should have a particular treatment, when the treatment itself could have an adverse effect on their quality of life. So, it isn't a question of ending their life: unless there is a genuine miracle, they are already going to die. It's a question of making their remaining time as good as it can be.

This is relatively easy to recognise with respect to examples like yet another round of chemotherapy, which would prolong life a little bit further, but which does not have the prospect of actually curing the patient. But one area which can be more controversial, and very painful for some patients and their loved ones, is when doctors decide that a patient should not be resuscitated if they go into cardiac arrest. People may feel that the medical team has 'written off' the patient or is unwilling to 'save their life'. And no doubt there have been times when some doctors have abusively made this decision, effectively as a way of committing euthanasia. However, it is important to note that CPR is itself a medical treatment. Indeed, it is a highly invasive and undignified treatment – and it is very often unsuccessful (whereas it is much more successful on TV, potentially creating unrealistic expectations).[7] Like any treatment, therefore, a doctor should not undertake CPR unless, to the best of their belief, it will actually be successful. When a doctor or medical team therefore decide that resuscitation is not in the patient's best interests, it should be based on their belief that it would not succeed, rather than because they think it would succeed but the patient's quality of life would be too low.

Another controversial example is that of withdrawing feeding and hydration from a patient. Some people understandably feel extremely nervous about withdrawing food and water from a sick person, because it feels like removing a basic human necessity rather than a medical treatment. But in the UK, since the tragic case of Tony Bland, feeding by tube and intravenous hydration are legally regarded as medical treatments, because they are *delivered* medically rather than in the normal way. Again, no doubt this is something

---

[7] See Susan J. Diem, et al, 'Cardiopulmonary Resuscitation on Television – Miracles and Misinformation', *New English Journal of Medicine* 334 (1996), pp. 1578–82, online at http://www.nejm.org/doi/full/10.1056/NEJM199606133342406#t=article.

which can be abused. It should never be done in order to end the life of a patient, or simply because the patient is dying and their quality of life has become extremely low. But when someone is dying, their kidneys and circulatory system may well lose their function before death. In such a case, the medical or palliative care team is faced with the difficult choice between withdrawing artificial hydration, which they know might hasten the patient's death or prolonging their life in a way which will cause their body to fill up with fluid which they cannot process, and which therefore also may hasten their death. In such a circumstance, it is entirely legitimate to withdraw the treatment, as the benefits are ambiguous at best. However, it must not be done in order to end the patient's life but in order to make their remaining time as comfortable as possible, even if this means not prolonging that time as much as they otherwise could.[8] So, there are times when treatment can legitimately be withdrawn or declined, without this amounting to euthanasia.

Tricky decisions 3: Pain relief which may hasten death

There's some debate about whether the same thing applies to some kinds of pain relief for

---

[8] This was actually not the case with Tony Bland, who was not dying and could still process fluids and food.

terminally ill patients suffering from extremely high levels of pain. In high enough doses, of course, morphine is lethal. And some have argued that the persistent use of morphine in high doses can hasten the end of life.[9]

Clearly, I am not qualified to judge this medical debate, although there is at least evidence to suggest that, responsibly used, morphine does not shorten life.[10] However, *even if* it was proven that the use of morphine was life-shortening, I still do not think people should feel guilty about using it as an analgesic. Just like any other medical treatment, responsibly used, it is taking the gifts of God in creation in order to alleviate suffering and therefore co-operates with God in God's kingdom work. The key point, once again, is not simply the consequence, but the reason that you use it. There is a big difference between deliberately taking (or administering) a lethal

---

[9] See the critique of this view by Dr Claude Regnard, a palliative care consultant, 'Double Effect is a Myth Leading a Double Life', *British Medical Journal*, 3 March 2007 (334), p. 440, online at http://www.ncbi.nlm.nih.gov/pmc/articles/PMC1808133/pdf/bmj-334-7591-ltr-0440c.pdf.

[10] See Tatsuya Morita et al, 'Effects of High Dose Opioids and Sedatives on Survival in Terminally Ill Cancer Patients', *Journal of Pain and Symptom Management*, 21.4 (2001), 282–9, online at http://www.jpsmjournal.com/article/S0885-3924(01)00258-5/pdf.

dose of morphine with the intention of ending
your or someone else's life, and taking a calcu-
lated dose in order to alleviate excruciating pain.
Even if you know that shortening life could be a
consequence, it is a side-effect rather than the
intended effect.[11]

Of course, this is not the only consideration
when using opiates for pain relief. For example,
a patient might choose not to use such high
doses of morphine that they would become unconscious, so that they have time consciously to
say goodbye to loved ones and make peace with
God before they die (although dying people often do become drowsy anyway). Good palliative
care specialists are well aware that these things
can be an important part of dying, and will work
to minimise pain and maximise consciousness
within what is possible in the circumstances.

Conclusions

As I close, I want to summarise the reasons why
deliberately taking human life (your own or another person's), or helping another person to end
their life, can never be the right thing to do.

1. As we've seen, human bodily life is created intrinsically good and precious by God. Being made in

---

[11] In the background again here is the principle
of double effect, which I discuss in more detail in
When Does Life Begin?

God's image, every person is special and irreplaceable. God has a purpose and calling for each of us, even in and through suffering. God does not want us to experience sickness and death, and he did not originally make us to suffer. This is why the Bible describes death as an 'enemy'. Therefore, we should gladly co-operate with Jesus in the ministry of healing, alleviating suffering whenever we can, but we should not collude with death by deliberately hastening it.

2. On the other hand, we cannot escape suffering, because humanity as a whole has rebelled against God's loving rule. Suffering is the consequence of turning away from a loving God and, therefore, whilst it is wonderful to heal sickness and alleviate pain wherever possible, it's rebellious to think we can always escape it or that we have the right to do so at all costs.

3. Only God can ultimately end suffering (and he has intervened to do so). It would be idolatrous to take his role away from him – and such idolatry tends to make things worse for us in the long run, not better.

4. There is always hope. Jesus shows us that God actually *wants* to heal people. So we can't assume that it is someone's time to die, still less speed someone on to their death, because there always remains the possibility of God's miraculous intervention. No sick person is beyond God's power and compassion. Instead of co-operating with death, we pray for healing and care for those who suffer, knowing that Jesus is full of compassion for the sick.

5. On the cross, God in Jesus is utterly present in the midst of suffering, pain and death. Far from compassion requiring the elimination of the sufferer, Jesus shows us the real meaning of compassion, which is literally 'suffering with'. He shares our bodily life and our suffering, he dignifies suffering with his presence – which is why Christians and many others have often noticed that God can be powerfully present even in the midst of the most horrific of realities. Of course, some people die without a conscious awareness of the presence of God. There is no guarantee whatsoever that death will feel like a spiritual experience, and it's not as if this in any way downplays the horror that it can be. But many people die with a profound sense of meeting with God and of knowing God's comfort and reassurance in their time of need and pain – because God has been there himself.

6. Just as, on the cross Jesus shows us what compassion really means, so he also shows us what it is to have true dignity in suffering. We should not be misled by the idea that 'dignity' in dying means being able to choose the manner and time of one's death. Every person *already has* dignity. It's a gift given to them by God which nothing can take away. Jesus died in unbearable physical agony and humiliating social shame and rejection. Yet who would dare mock him for the lack of dignity in his death? Or to put it another way, Christ has entered into the indignity of suffering and death and dignified it with his presence. Although it is right to

pray and long for healing, we know from the cross that the power and victory of the Kingdom is not only a matter of forcible intervention. It also comes through endurance, just as God's own victory came through enduring the agony of the cross. So, even if God does not heal someone, and even if medicine cannot help them, that doesn't mean that they are beyond hope and grace. Again, this will make us cautious about enabling someone to die early, because God could meet them in their time of suffering and bring good things from it. This doesn't mean that he sends the pain in order to bring good things from it. But the cross of Jesus Christ shows us that God can redeem it.

I'd like to end with a real example of this. A couple of years ago, I spoke on this subject at a conference and I was privileged that a woman came up to me afterwards to share her story. Indeed, she asked me to share it with others too, and I'm grateful for her encouragement to do so. Her mother-in-law, who was not a Christian, had been diagnosed with motor neurone disease, and had begged her daughter-in-law to help her go to the Dignitas Clinic in Switzerland to end her life. The woman loved her mother-in-law deeply and hated to see her suffer. She was sorely tempted to help her mother-in-law do this. But in the end she could not bring herself to do it. Instead, she looked after her mother-in-law as best she could, and invited her to receive regular prayer for healing in a Christian healing centre. In one sense, her mother-in-law was not miraculously healed, and sadly she eventually died. But two things did happen. First, she experienced a measure of relief from her physical suffering as a result of prayer. Second, impacted by the faithful care and love she received from her daughter-in-law and at the healing centre, she became a Christian before she died. Her daughter-in-law looked me straight in the eye and asked me, 'What if I had taken her to Zurich?'

Go Deeper

Nigel Biggar, *Aiming to Kill: The Ethics of Suicide and Euthanasia* (London: DLT, 2004).
CMF, 'Life is Precious: Michael' video online at https://www.youtube.com/watch?v=HwbiDYq Pn0g.
Michael Wenham, *My Donkey Body: Living with a Body that No Longer Obeys You!* (Oxford: Monarch, 2008).

The Only Way is Ethics
Part 1: Sex and Marriage

ISBN 978-1-78078-144-0

Available as a collection or individual chapters

Living Out My Story

And some pastoral and missional thoughts about homosexuality along the way

ISBN 978-1-78078-147-1 978-1-78078-436-6 (e-book)

QUILTBAG

Jesus and Sexuality

ISBN 978-1-78078-146-4 978-1-78078-435-9 (e-book)

Sexual Singleness

Why singleness is good, and practical thoughts on being single and sexual

ISBN 978-1-78078-148-8 978-1-78078-437-3 (e-book)

As Long as You Love Me

Divorce and remarriage

ISBN 978-1-78078-149-5 978-1-78078-438-0 (e-book)

Lightning Source UK Ltd.
Milton Keynes UK
UKOW06f1201210716

278922UK00001B/37/P